MY ANIMAL KINGDOM

ALL ABOUT ZEBRAS

DeAGOSTINI

Dear Friend,

Welcome to My Animal Kingdom!

My name's Zak and I'm a zebra. I'm here, together with my young son Zane, to tell you about our life on the plains of Africa. You're going to find out all about where we live, what we eat and why we go on long journeys.

Did you know that we live in herds? Or that we like nothing better than rolling in the dust? There are lots of fascinating zebra facts to discover and you'll have great fun meeting my family and friends.

I hope you have a great time as you follow me through this book!

Zak

CONTENTS

Let's trot through the pages!

Zebras look like small, stripy horses. They are the wild horses of Africa. Under their stripy skins, zebras are very like their tame cousins. They have sturdy, barrel-shaped bodies and short manes on the upper part of their necks. Their strong legs are built for running and their hooved feet help them to speed across the grasslands.

I use my long tail to flick away flies.

My barrel-shaped stomach can hold lots of grass.

Black and white rules!

Tough hooves protect my feet. They're great for running on hard surfaces.

4

ZEBRA FACTS

NAME: Equus burchelli (common or plains zebra)
ANIMAL GROUP: mammal
ANIMAL FAMILY: Equidae (horses, zebras and asses)
COLOUR: black or brown with white stripes

SIZE: body length of 2–2.5 m and up to 1.4 m tall at the shoulder
WEIGHT: 300–400 kg
SPEED: up to 65 km/h
EATS: grasses
DRINKS: water
LIVES: up to 28 years

— My striped mane stands upright.

STUNNING STRIPES

DID YOU KNOW?

- No two zebras have the same pattern of stripes.
- Zebras probably recognize each other by their stripy patterns. A mother zebra recognizes her baby from its coat pattern and its smell.
- The zebra's stripes help to break up the outline of its body. This makes it hard for a hunter to pick out any one zebra from the herd.

My eyes are spaced far apart to help me to spot danger from all round.

I have strong legs to help me run long distances.

5

Zebras have large, upright ears and big eyes. They can swivel their ears to pick up sounds from all round them. Their eyes are set on either side of their head, so they can see all round, too. The zebra's good hearing, sight and sense of smell help it to detect danger, and warn it to run away.

HARD HOOVES

Zebras walk on the tips of their toes. Each foot has just one, large, middle toe protected by a hard hoof. A hoof is like a thick, wrap-around toenail. It is made of the same, hard stuff, called keratin, as your nails. A zebra's hooves never wear out. Like your fingernails, they keep on growing throughout a zebra's life.

TOUGH TEETH

A zebra's teeth are great for munching grass. The front teeth, or incisors, are like pincers. The zebra uses them to nip off juicy grass stems. Then it uses its flat cheek teeth to crush the stems. This grinding action wears the teeth down. But a zebra's cheek teeth keep on growing all its life.

I can turn my large ears to pick up the smallest sounds.

My eyes are on either side of my head. I can see to the side and behind me as well as in front.

I have a good sense of smell. I can sniff out my friends and my enemies.

What a smart set stripes!

WHERE I LIVE

Common zebras, like Zak and Zane, live on the grasslands, or savannah, of Africa. It is hot and dry on the savannah, especially in the summer. Zebras need a long drink at least once a day. This means that they never travel too far from rivers or water-holes.

WHERE IN THE WORLD?

There are three kinds, or species, of zebra. They live only in Africa. The common, or plains, zebra lives in southern and eastern Africa. The mountain zebra lives in south-west Africa and Grevy's zebra lives in eastern Africa and Ethiopia. Other wild horses are found only in Africa and Asia. Domesticated horses, and horses that are descended from tame horses but now run wild, live all over the world.

That's where we live!

AFRIC

SUPER STRIPES

The largest of the zebras, Grevy's zebras, live in semi-desert areas. These zebras have even more stripes than their common cousins. Grevy's zebras don't form mixed herds like other zebras. Instead adult males live alone. Females and their young live in small herds, as do young males.

MEETING PLACE

DID YOU KNOW?

Zebras often drink at dawn and dusk. They meet up with other grazing animals at the water-hole. All the animals keep a lookout for predators and warn each other if danger threatens. The more eyes there are the better!

9

Over 300,000 common zebras live on African grasslands. They share their home with lots of other plant eaters. Luckily, not all the animals eat the same plants, so there is enough food for them all. Many grazers travel together, moving from place to place. This gives the grass time to grow back in one area while the animals feed in another.

His horns are longer than my stripes, Dad!

HARD HORNS

An oryx, like this one, is not a fussy feeder. It can chew up coarse grass and will even feed on thorny shrubs. Like all antelopes, the oryx can speed away if danger threatens. It can also give a nasty wound with its long, spear-like horns. They can be up to a metre long!

'TOUGH OX'

Hartebeests often graze with zebras, wildebeest and gazelles. This odd-looking antelope enjoys nibbling juicy, young grasses. It also chews up dry grasses that other grazers don't want. A hartebeest can run for hours without getting tired. That's why it's called a hartebeest or 'tough ox'!

BIRD WATCHERS

Zebras and other animals often graze near ostriches. At over two metres tall, the ostrich is a great lookout. With its huge eyes it can spot predators from a long way away and hiss a warning.

Common zebras live in family herds of up to six females and their young. The group has one adult male, or stallion. His job is to defend the herd. Sometimes several family herds join together to form big herds on the plains. Zebras can always recognize each other by their coat patterns, sounds and smell.

Zane's mum, Zandra, is my chief mare. She and Zane lead the rest of the herd when we travel to new feeding grounds. I keep lookout at the back.

This is little Zane. I'd recognize those stripes anywhere!

Look at Zane's older sisters Zara and Zelda! They're great friends and often play and rest together.

These two young stallions, Zee and Zebedee, are always fighting! They are trying to see who's strongest by squealing, kicking and biting!

13

Zebras usually have their babies in the spring. Newborn zebra foals have longer, furrier coats and a short body with long legs. They are almost a metre tall and weigh about 30 kilograms – that's about as much as a seven-year-old child. The zebra mother keeps her newborn baby close by her side. She does not let the other mares get too near. This may give the foal time to learn its mother's pattern of stripes.

WOBBLY WALKING

Newborn zebras don't have time to lie around. They take their first wobbly steps within an hour. By the time they are a few hours old, they can run with Mum and the herd.

BABY FILE

BIRTH

Female zebras usually have one foal a year. Mum looks after her baby, guarding it against hunters such as lions. At first, the baby foal only drinks its mum's milk.

THREE MONTHS

The foal grows fast. It still drinks its mum's milk but it can now eat grass, too. The foal grazes with the herd but will stay with Mum until her next baby is born.

ONE TO TWO YEARS

The foal is almost fully grown. It can take care of itself. After two years, young males leave to form groups on their own. Some females also leave to form a herd with a young stallion.

MUD BATH

A zebra doesn't clean itself by washing. Instead it rolls in mud or dust. When the mud dries, the zebra has a good shake. The mud falls off, taking loose hair and dry skin with it. A roll in the dust gets rid of nasty, biting bugs, too.

THE LONG JOURNEY

It doesn't rain much during the dry season on the African savannah. Many water-holes dry up and the grass turns yellow and dies. There is so little food that many common zebras have to travel long distances to find new feeding grounds. If they don't, they will starve. Thousands of wildebeest and antelope join the zebras on their long journey.

REAR GUARD

Even when they are travelling with other animals, zebras keep in their family herds. They walk in a line with the chief female and her foal at the front. The stallion stays at the back as a guard.

WILD WATERS

The long journey that the zebras go on is full of dangers. They have to cross rivers where hungry crocodiles lie in wait. The zebras jump into the water and swim as fast as they can to the other side. Most of them make it. But if it can, the crafty crocodile will grab an animal by the leg and pull it beneath the water to drown it.

Wait for me, Dad!

Like a domesticated horse, a zebra's favourite food is grass. It grazes on all kinds of grass, including tough, dry stalks. But grass doesn't contain a lot of goodness. So zebras have to eat plenty of it to stay healthy. They nibble away for up to 16 hours a day!

I love nibbling juicy grass shoots.

GRASS GUZZLER

WELL DIGGER

Zebras can live without water for up to three days. But they really like to have a drink every day. If they can't find water, zebras sometimes dig for it. They use their front hooves to dig wells up to a metre deep.

Zebras like to snack on fresh grass shoots. But they usually have to make do with older, tough stalks. If there is not enough grass around, zebras will gobble up leaves, other plant shoots and fruit. They nip off the food with their front teeth, and then grind it to a pulp with their cheek teeth.

GRAZERS AND BROWSERS

More than 40 kinds of browsing and grazing animal live on the African savannah. But they all eat different parts of various plants, so no one goes hungry. Grazers such as zebras, gazelles and buffalo eat different parts, or growth stages, of the grasses. Browsers such as giraffes and antelope prefer to munch up shrubs and bushes, or to strip juicy leaves from trees.

The animals of the African savannah are divided into two groups – the hunters and the hunted. And zebras are hunted! A zebra makes a tasty meal that will feed a whole pride of lions. So zebras must be on their guard day and night. That's why they live in herds. Lots of pairs of eyes keeping watch for hungry predators are better than just one pair.

BEWARE! LIONS

The lion is one of the zebra's most dangerous enemies. Lions are cunning carnivores that hunt in packs. The lionesses stalk their prey at dusk. When they are close, they form a circle around their target. They often single out one particular zebra, then they attack.

Run!

ON GUARD

Zebras have lots of tricks to foil predators. They can run fast and they can kick very hard, too. And their stripes help! It is difficult for a hunter to pick out a single zebra from a herd of stripes!

FOOD CHAINS

The animals and plants on the savannah are linked by the foods they eat. For example, grass, a zebra and a leopard are linked because the zebra eats the grass then the leopard eats the zebra. These links are called food chains.

21

A DAY IN MY LIFE

6:00 AM

The sun was just rising. We had moved during the night and I'd managed to find some good grass to munch on.

8:00 AM

We met some giraffes and wildebeest down at the water-hole. After drinking, we all moved off together to graze nearby. It's safer to be in a big group.

12 NOON

It was hot, so we moved into the shade of some trees to keep cool. I flicked away the flies with my tail. Zane settled down to sleep.

2:00 PM

I felt quite sleepy and dozed off, too. There were some ostriches nearby and I knew they would soon warn us if there was any danger about.

5:00 PM

It was cooler and the young foals played a game of tag while we kept watch.

6:00 PM

The sun was beginning to sink in the sky. We made our way down to the river for a long, cool drink.

8:00 PM

We were grazing peacefully when I suddenly heard a sound in the undergrowth – lions! I snorted and barked to warn the others and we raced away.

9:00 PM

Safe again. There had been three lionesses but they gave up the chase. I'd stayed at the back as we ran, ready to lash out with a kick if they got too close.

12:00 MIDNIGHT

We found some nice, juicy grass and settled down to eat and fill our stomachs again! I heard a leopard in the distance but it didn't come near us.

4:00 AM

We had a peaceful night grazing and dozing. Not long until morning. I think I'll just have a few more mouthfuls of grass to keep me going!

Zak

The horse family includes zebras, horses and asses. Ten thousand years ago there were many different types of wild horse, living all over the world. Now, true wild members of the horse family are found only in parts of Asia and Africa.

> He'd look better if he combed his hair.

PRZEWALSKI'S HORSE

Przewalski's horse is the only true wild horse left in the world. It is a small, plump horse with a mane that sticks up like a brush. In the wild, these horses live in the deserts of Mongolia. But more of these horses are kept in zoos than live in the wild!

24

ANCIENT TAPIR

Tapirs are distant relatives of the zebra. They look a bit like hairy pigs with short trunks. In fact, tapirs look the same today as they did almost 35 million years ago! They live in rain-forests in South America and Asia.

DID YOU KNOW?

● The horse family belongs to a group of animals called perissodactyls. These are hooved animals that have an odd number of toes. This group includes horses, tapirs and rhinoceroses.

● One of the first horses, Eohippus, lived more than 50 million years ago. It was only the size of a greyhound.

ASIAN ASS

The onager is an Asian wild ass. It lives in groups led by the chief male. Onagers like to eat all kinds of grass, from juicy, new shoots to tough, dry stems. In summer, the onager feeds high up on the hillsides. But in winter, the herds move down into the warmer valleys.

Zebras cannot be tamed. But their cousins, horses, can. The first wild horses were tamed about 6,500 years ago. Since then, people have trained them to do many jobs – from pulling carts to carrying soldiers to war. Today, there are over 100 breeds of tame horse in the world.

RACING

Horses are used in many sports, such as showjumping, racing and polo. Champion race horses can be worth millions of pounds. And their owners can win thousands of pounds if the horse comes first in a famous race!

ZOO ZEBRAS

Today, many zebras are kept in zoos all over the world. People like to look at these stripy animals. But native farmers used to think that zebras were pests. They ate the grass they needed for their cattle. So the farmers shot large numbers of zebras. Many kinds of zebra are now under threat. There are only 1,500 Grevy's zebras left in the wild.

I'll race you to the water-hole, Zane!

DID YOU KNOW?

● Two kinds of zebra have died out in the past 150 years.
● In Ancient Rome, the zebra was called a 'horse tiger' and was used as a circus animal.
● Domestic horses are measured in hands. One hand equals 10 centimetres. A zebra would be about 14 hands high.

WHAT DOES IT MEAN?

ANTELOPE
Deer-like animals, such as gazelles, impala and hartebeests, that are found in Africa and India.

ASS
A group of animals in the horse family. Domesticated asses are commonly known as donkeys.

DESCENDED
To have come down from something. To be descended from someone means that you are in the same family as them but you live at a later time. You are their descendant. They are your ancestor. Today's domestic horses are descended from wild horses.

DOMESTICATED
An animal that has been trained, or tamed, to live with people.

FOIL
To frustrate, confuse or defeat something such as a plan.

SNICKER
A whinny or a neigh.

WHINNY
A gentle or happy neighing sound.